Royalists, Roundheads, and Rogues,

their connections with Reigate in
the 17th Century.

i

REDHILL CENTRE

FOR

&*Local Family History*

ISBN 0-9537532-2-0

Although every attempt has been made to check the information contained in this book, the Publishers are not responsible for its content or accuracy.

Digitally Printed from Copy Supplied by Parchment (Oxford) Ltd
Printworks, Crescent Road, Cowley, Oxford, England OX4 2PB

Published by: Redhill Centre for Local & Family History
Redhill Library, Warwick Quadrant
Redhill, Surrey, RH1 1NN
Tel. no. 01737 773204 Fax no. 01737 778020
e-mail: redhill.centre@surreycc.gov.uk
http://www.surreyweb.org.uk/redhill-history-centre

Introduction

Some years ago I was asked to research the Earl of Holland's rising and Reigate's part in it. It was hoped to re-enact events on the 350th anniversary in an attempt to raise money for local charities.

Unfortunately, the standard answer to my enquiries was "Your wasting your time, nothing ever happened in Reigate", this made me all the more determined to prove people wrong and I went further afield in my search. However, as often happens in these cases, the project fell through due to local apathy and indifference and I was left with boxes of notes that I didn't know what to do with.

These papers remained filed and gathering dust until last year when I was asked to write something for the Heritage Project.

I had just been told that 17th century history was no longer taught in our local schools, so I decided to unearth my notes and before the names of Howard and Peterborough, Monson and Mordaunt fade completely from peoples' memories share with you some of the events of that turbulent time.

You never know, you might be in for a few surprises, Reigate wasn't such a quiet place as you thought, quite a lot of things actually did happen here!

BMP
June 2000

iii

Contents

1

Illustration Acknowledgements

The Author is grateful to the following Institutions and Libraries for permission to reproduce their illustrations.

British Museum Page 5 Ref. PS 189545. Ilustrations on Pages 15, 35 and 65 Refs. PX 122/11, PX122/27 and PX/122 are reproduced by permission of Surrey History Service.
Hodder Children's Books for the Title Page and Page 47 which appear in The Picture Reference book of the Early Stuarts. printed by Brockhampton Press, 1969.
The Parish Office for the picture of the church of St. Mary Magdelen, Reigate on page 77.

Illustrations

The Admiral

Charles Howard, Earl of Nottingham by T. Cockson

Author's Notes

Until 1752 the new year began on the 25th March,
any dates mentioned that fall during the first 3 months
are shown with both years ie. 3rd March 1647/8
which is by our reckoning 3rd March 1648.
Spelling had not been standardised and was still
very much up to an individual own preference.
Text shown in *Italics* is in the original 17th
century spelling and may appear rather strange
to the present day reader.
Parish Registers referred to in this book can be
consulted in numerous places, The Surrey History
Centre, Woking; The Society of Genealogists,
Goswell Road, London, EC1M; The Family Record
Centre, Myddelton Street, London, EC1R and in the
case of St. Mary's Reigate, at the Family and Local
History Centre, Redhill Library.

At the beginning of the 17th century, Reigate Priory was owned by a member of the powerful Howard family. Once more in their sovereign's favour after the disasters of the previous century when the family rose too far too fast, providing two Queens of England. Anne Boleyn and Catherine Howard both lost their heads through extra marital indiscretions, as did Henry Howard, the poet Earl of Surrey.

His father Thomas, Duke of Norfolk, was only saved from a similar fate by the timely death of the King, Henry VIII. Whilst not the favourite home of its owner Charles Howard, Earl of Nottingham and Lord Admiral of England, it provided a pleasant country retreat where he could escape from the rigours of Court life and entertain his friends. Close enough to London for a speedy return when his Queen and kinswoman Elizabeth required his presence. Indeed it was while attending the Queen at Richmond that the Admiral had news of his wife's final illness and death in February 1602/3.

Catherine, the Countess of Nottingham was also kin to the Queen, her grandfather William Carey had married Mary Boleyn . Mary had been Henry's mistress before her sister Anne had caught the King's eye on her return from France.

William and Mary's son Henry, named for the King to whom he had a more than passing resemblance, was therefore Elizabeth's cousin, or as some said, her half-brother. Henry was created Lord Hunsdon and his daughter Catherine became one of the Queen's Ladies in Waiting before marrying Charles Howard.

Every schoolboy knows the story of the Countess and the Earl of Essex's ring. It was said that at some time in their tempestuous relationship Elizabeth I had given Essex a ring, telling him, that if ever he was in peril of his life, to return it to her and she would save him.

In 1600 after his disasterous adventures in Ireland, with mounting debts the Earl appealed to the Queen for help. Elizabeth, however, set a price on her assistance, which, in his increasing state of meglomania, Essex refused to meet, saying before witnesses that:

".....her conditions were as crooked as her carcass."

A comment not likely to endear him to the ageing Queen. His behaviour became more erratic with each passing day and with the ever present threat of bankruptcy, the desperate Earl put the wrong interpretation on vague grumblings of dissatisfaction in the country. He conceived a plan with the Earl of Southampton to overthrow Elizabeth, backed by popular support.

But once again the Earl had misjudged the situation. Moaning about the Queen and the upper classes was something of a national pastime, the majority of the population were very proud of Elizabeth, no matter how much they mumbled in their ale.

The popular support he had expected was not forthcoming and the coupe failed miserably. Both Essex and Southampton were arrested and charged with treason, found guilty with the dreadful prospect of being hung, drawn and quartered, the desperate Essex sent a messenger with instructions to give Elizabeth's ring to Lady Scrope who would intercede with the Queen on his behalf. Unfortunately for the Earl, his messenger made a disastrous mistake, he gave the ring to the Countess of Nottingham, wife of the Earl's old enemy, the Lord Admiral, instead of her sister.

Lady Catherine like a dutiful wife, reported the matter to her husband who decided to do nothing.

Essex was granted a stay of execution, perhaps the Queen hoped he would return her ring so that she would have an excuse to forgive him, as she had done so many times in the past, but no plea for mercy came and on Shrove Tuesday the 24th February 1600/1, Elizabeth was persuaded to sign the Earl's death warrant

On Ash Wednesday, within the confines of the Tower, Essex was beheaded at the age of 34.

Elizabeth's final gift to her foolish and unappreciative favourite, a clean , quick death by the headsman, instead of being drawn on a hurdle to Tyburn, disembowelled whilst still alive and having head, arms and legs cut off and displayed at various vantage points about the Capital.

When the Countess of Nottingham was taken ill at Richmond in February 1602/3 she is said to have confessed to the Queen her part in the affair, where- upon Elizabeth flew into a towering rage saying,

" God may forgive you but I never will."

Unfortunately, this part of the legend does not stand close scrutiny. The Countess died at Arundell House on the Strand and the entry in the Chelsea Parish Register reads:

[1]

"Catharyn, the Countess of Nottinham died the 25th day of February, at Arondell-howse, London and buried at Chelsey, the 28th day of the same,whose funeralls were fonourably kepte at Chelsey 21st day of March 1603."

Although the Countess was not buried in the Howard vault at Reigate, John Hampton, the vicar, who was also the Admiral's chaplain noted in the registers of St. Mary Magdalene:

> " 1602/3 ffebruary the xxv day beinge fryday [2]
> departed the life of the righte honorable the
> Lady Catheren howard, Countess of
> Nottingham late wiffe to the righte honorable
> Lord highe Admirall of England wch Countis
> was buryed at Chelsey the monday night
> folowinge being xxvii february And being
> Layed in the earth at Chelsey her funerall was
> at Chelsey kept the xxi of March beinge
> monday, and she dyed at Arundell house in
> London."

Legends aside, the Queen took her cousin's death very hard, falling into a deep melancholy. She had retreated to Richmond *"the warm winter box to shelter her old age"* and not even a visit from Sir Robert Carey, Lord Hunsdon's youngest son could cheer her.

By the second week in March her health had deteriorated and it was obvious to all that the end was not far off.

She was suffering from insomnia and had refused to go to bed, laying instead on cushions on the floor of her Presence Chamber. But, by the 23rd of March when she was so weak she had lost the power of speech she finally allowed her ladies to put her to bed.

It was at this point as she lay *"in extremis"* her ministers crowding round her bed, that Lord Cecil voiced the question they had all been afraid to ask, who was to succeed her, but she was to weak to answer him. He repeated the question saying...

3

> *"... does your Majesty remain in your*
> *former resolutions and that you would*
> *have the King of Scots to succeed you*
> *in your Kingdom, show some sign unto us ? "*

She managed to raise her hand in assent but, with this action it was as though all her strength had drained from her wasted body. She fell into a deep sleep, the first time for nearly a week, a sleep from which she never woke, dying at 3 a.m. on Tuesday 24th March.

The Admiral took his wife's death *"exceeding grieveously"* keeping to his chamber *" mourning in sad earnest"*. Whether this show of grief was entirely genuine or had more to do with the Earl's uncertainty as to the Queen's reaction to his wife's confession is hard to say. However by June 1604 he had cast aside his mourning and married again at the age of 67.

His youthful bride was Margaret, the daughter of James Stewart, Earl of Murray.

The Registers show several children were born to the couple in the years that followed:

4

> *" 1608 Nov the xi daie was borne a Sonne*
> *of the Right Hon. Charles Howard and*
> *Lady Margaret his wife".*

11

The following day:

"1608   Nov the xii daie was buryed
A Sonne of the Ryght honourable
Charles howard, Earle of Nottingham
and Margaret his wife. "[5]

James, buried June 5, 1610[6]

"William, the sonne of Charles Howard,
Lord Admiral was baptized Dec. 5 1617."[7]
Buried at Chelsea two days later.

" Margaret the daughter of the Earl of
Nottingham , was baptized Dec. 22 1618"[8]

Of all the children born to the Admiral and Lady
Margaret only one son survived to maturity.
Charles , born 25th December 1610, who was to
become the third Earl of Nottingham, but like his half-
brother, another Charles, he was also to die childless in
1681, the title passing to a junior branch of the family.
With the arrival of the new King from Scotland,
the Admiral was kept busy. In May 1603 he was
appointed to the Commission for overseeing
preparations for the forthcoming coronation. In 1604 he
became a Commissioner for negotiating the peace with
Spain and in the following year he was made
Ambassador Extraordinary to ratify the terms of the
peace agreement. With an allowance of £15,000, a
fabulous sum in those days and 500 retainers, the
gentlemen of his personal staff, all in black velvet cloaks,
the Admiral made a lasting impression on the Spaniards.

The King of Spain was so pleased with the English embassy that he undertook to be responsible for paying for all their food and transport.

Before his return to England, the Admiral was heaped with presents of plate, jewels and horses said to value over £20,000.

On her marriage to Frederick the Elector Palatine on the 14th February 1612/13, Princess Elizabeth was conducted to the altar by the Earl and the Duke of Lennox. After the ceremony, the 76 year old Admiral escorted the Princess and her husband to Flushing on their return journey to the Palatinate, no mean feat for a man of his age.

The Admiral continued in royal favour during his remaining years, acting as Lord Lieutenant of Surrey.

He died at his favourite residence of Haling House, near Croydon, on the 14th December 1624 aged 88.

[9]

"The xviii daie of December at night
was buried the Right Honourable
Charles, Earl of Nottingham..."

The Admiral chose as his final resting place the quiet country town were he had spent many a pleasant day, when his duties allowed. He was buried in the Howard family vault at the Parish Church of St. Mary Magdalene rather than with his first wife, Lady Catherine at Chelsea.

Sources

1. Parish Registers, Chelsea.
2. Parish Registers. Reigate.
3. Public Record Office, Kew.
4. Parish Registers, Reigate.
5. Parish Registers, Reigate.
6. Parish Registers, Chelsea.
7. Parish Registers, Chelsea.
8. Parish Registers, Chelsea.
9. Parish Registers, Reigate

The Regicide

South view of Reigate Priory from an engraving dated 1785, little has changed from the previous century.

Copyright of Surrey History Service

Author's Notes

There has been a great deal of discussion in recent years as to the parentage of the **Monson** who marries the Admiral's widow. Both **Thomas** and **William Monson** the Admiral's contemporarys had sons called **William** and while **Dr. Hooper** chose the **Admiral William** who lived at **Kinnersley Manor** as the father, I think, after extensive research, that it was more likely his elder brother **Thomas**, who was married to **Margaret Anderson.** A fact that has now been confirmed by the Surrey History Centre at Working

William Monson was born at Burton in the county of Lincolnshire, probably about 1601. His father was Thomas Monson, son of Sir John Monson and Jane Dighton his wife, who had married Margaret Anderson daughter of Edmund Anderson, Lord Chief Justice of Common Pleas and his wife, Magdelena Smith.

Both William's father and uncle, Admiral Sir William Monson, were suspected of being involved in the murder of Sir Thomas Overbury, and the Admiral spent some time in the Tower but was released in July 1616 as nothing could be proved.

In 1627 William married Margaret, the widow of Charles Howard, the Earl of Nottingham. The wedding took place in the chapel of Reigate Priory, the bride's home, with John Hampton, the Nottingham's family chaplain officiating.

The following year 1628 their son, Stewart, was born, sadly the babe only lived a few days and was buried at Chelsea on the 8th April.

Less than a year later William was raised to the peerage of Ireland as Viscount Monson of Castlemaine and on the 13th August 1633 he was knighted. On that day he also became a member of Grays Inn.

Not a popular man with the locals, he tried to reinstate the custom which gave the Lord of Reigate the right to hunt over his tenants' lands. A move which involved him in litigation on several fronts. He also, in his wife's name, cut down trees on three local commons together with a number of oaks in the Priory Park, with the intent of turning the land into rabbit warrens.

In 1637/8 when Charles I was short of money to pay the navy, he introduced a tax called 'Ship Money' which proved very unpopular. Like many another country gentleman, William Monson refused to pay, he was as usual, deeply in debt, owing to his lavish lifestyle.

His affairs took a turn for the worse in August 1639, when his wife Margaret, died.

> *"The Ritte Hon. Margaret, Countess of Nottinghame, died on the 4th day of August, in Common* (Covent) *Garden, London and was buried heare at Chelsea the 19th day of the same month. 1639."* [1]

The Priory, which was held by Lady Margaret for her lifetime, reverted to her step grand-daughter, Elizabeth, Countess of Peterborough. Unfortunately for the Mordaunts, Lord Monson had grown used to having the revenues from the estate and refused to give up the Priory. He was taken to Court by the Countess but it was many years before she gained possession of her inheritance.

At the outbreak of the Civil War, Lord Monson, who had received many honours from the King, supported neither party and was known in Parliament as an Independent.

In May 1646 William Monson married again. His wife was Frances, the daughter of Thomas Alston of Polstead in Suffolk. This union produced an heir, Alston, who died in 1674 without issue. This marriage did not last long, by 1653 Frances was dead.

In a petition to Cromwell in 1654, Monson pleads:

2

> *"... as my son is only 7 years old, I cannot dispose of any part of the estate either to pay my debts or provide for my younger children."*

None of these 'younger children' survived to maturity.

In 1648 with the war having gone against the King, William Monson saw a way to pay off his mounting debts. He started to confiscate property from his Royalist neighbours. A letter dated July of that year from the Committee of both Houses at Derby House warned him that such behaviour would not be tolerated.

3

> *" We are informed that your Lordship is proceeding to the sequestration of some of the inhabitants about Reigate who are now attending here by order of this Committee. We conceive it fit to for bear that proceeding till they be first heard, and if there be cause of sequestration that it be done by the whole Committee of the County meeting at Kingston for that purpose. We are also informed that your castle is garrisoned at the charge of the country, wherrby the people are much discontented and then disaffection.*

*We hope there will be no need to
keep a garrison there, especially if
the place be made indefensible
according to the order of the House
of Commons, which we desire to take
care to see executed, and that there be
no further charge upon the County for
the keeping of it."*

Monson took little notice of the order from the Committee to make Reigate castle indefensible. When the Royalists under the command of the Earl of Holland arrived of the 6th July 1648, they found no resistance. However, they only held the castle for a few hours before the arrival of Major Lewis Audeley and the forces of Parliament under the overall command of Sir Michael Livesey. With the departure of the fleeing Royalists, Sir Michael left a garrison of 20 men under Mr. Fenneck to hold the castle until his return.

Lord Monson had little time to worry about the state of his castle in January 1648/9, he was nominated as one of the King's judges by Parliament, but only attended the proceedings on three days before refusing to take any further part. He was, however, one of the signatories of the King's death warrant.

In July 1649 pressing debts forced him to try and persuade Parliament that he was owed £4,500, arrears of the pension due to his first wife, Margaret, Countess of Nottingham. Parliament was not convinced and he lost the motion by two votes.

In 1654 sometime after his wife Frances' death, Lord Monson married for a third time. Elizabeth Reresby was the daughter of a Yorkshire Knight, George Reresby of Thybergh.

She had been married twice before, firstly to Sir Francis Foljambe, bart. of Aldwick, and on his death to Edward Horner, youngest son of Sir John Horner of Mells in Somerset. The new Lady Monson was not made in the mould of the usually submissive 17th century wife. According to gossip she had a mind and inheritance of her own and was not above laying violent hands on her erring husband if she thought he deserved it.

Somehow they stopped fighting long enough to produce a daughter, Elizabeth, who married into another Yorkshire family when she became the wife of Sir Philip Hungate, bart., of Saxton.

In 1659 when the Long Parliament was restored, its members were obliged to send an order to the Fleet Prison for the release of William Monson and Henry Martin in order that they might form a legal quorum. Both men had been imprisoned for debt , but Parliament, however much it disliked the action was forced to procure their release.

On the Restoration of Charles II in 1660 there came a time to settle old scores. William Monson, Viscount Castlemain, was excepted from the bill of general pardon and on 21st June was once more committed to the Fleet.

Unlike many of the surviving Regicides, Monson escaped the dreadful punishment which was his due for committing treason.

On the 1st July 1661 he was brought once more from the Fleet to the House of Commons and after confessing his crime was stripped of his titles and estates. Instead of being hung, drawn and quartered, the now plain William Monson, traitor and regicide, was sentenced to be drawn from the Tower, through the City of London to Tyburn, on a hurdle with a halter round his neck and thence back again.

This degrading journey took place every year until his death, on the anniversary of the sentencing of the King. Pepys writes in his diary of February 27th 1661/62 ...

[4]

> *"This morning, going to take water upon Tower-hill, we met three sleddes standing to carry my Lord Monson, and Sir H. Mildmay and another (* Robert Wallop) *to the gallows and back again, with ropes about their necks; this to be repeated every year, this being the day of their sentencing the King."*

William Monson died in the Fleet prison sometime in 1672 and his Reigate estate had already been given to James, Duke of York, the King's brother.

His widow Elizabeth married for the fourth time and thanks to her Reresby relations was able to regain her title of Viscountess Castlemaine.

This title was later to become notorious when Charles II bestowed it on his mistress Barbara, the wife of Roger Palmer, known throughout history as the notorious Lady Castlemaine.

Sources

1. Parish Registers, Chelsea.
2. Calendar of State Papers. Domestic.
3. Calendar of State Papers. Domestic.
4. Samuel Pepys' Diary.

The Countess

The Great Fireplace, Reigate Priory

25

Author's Notes

The carved fire surround shown in the
illustration on the previous page was
removed from Blechingley Place and
installed in Reigate Priory by Elizabeth,
the Dowager Countess of Peterborough
in 1655. It can still be seen by visitors
to the Priory Museum which is open
on Wednesday and Saturday afternoons
during term time.

On a cold February day in 1596/7 Chelsea witnessed the wedding of the Lord Admiral 's heir, William Howard, who married Agnes St. John, or, as the entry in the parish register reads:

[1]

> " *Dnus. Willmus Howarde et Agneta St. John,*
> *filia et haeres Dni. St. John de Bletsoe,*
> *traxerunt matrimonium 7th die Februarii 1696/7.*"

The young couple were to spend most of their early married life at Blechingley Place, the house given them by William's father, but it was at Arundell House on the Strand that their daughter Elizabeth was born and baptised. The birth of the Admiral's grand-daughter was noted by William Cawsey, vicar of Reigate:

[2]

> "*1602/3 February the vii day was baptised*
> *Elizabeth, the daughter of the Right*
> *honourable Willia. Lord Howard of*
> *Effingham, wch sayd Elizabeth was borne*
> *the xixth day of Janua. last before at*
> *Arundell house in London and there also*
> *baptised.*"

Rejoicing at the babe's safe delivery was cut short by the illness and then death of her grand-mother Catherine on the 25th February, followed by the country's mourning on the death of her namesake, Queen Elizabeth in March.

In October 1605 the couple once more made the journey to Chelsea, this time the event was a happier one, the baptism of another daughter, Ann.

" Anna, filia Dni. de Effingham et Anna
uxoris, baptiz. 12 Octobris 1605". [3]

Less than a month after the christening, a large number of barrels filled with gunpowder together with an even larger pile of firewood was discovered in the cellars of the Houses of Parliament.

A plot to blow up King James, his family and most of his court was narrowly averted, thus saving the lives of Charles Howard, the Admiral and his son William who would have been in attendance on the King when he went to open Parliament.

In the aftermath of the near tragedy, feelings ran high against the Catholic minority and the Admiral was appointed to the Commission responsible for trying those concerned with the plot. One of whom was Elizabeth's future father-in-law, the 4th Lord Mordaunt, who spent more than a year in the Tower under suspicion. When he died in 1608 shortly after his release King James removed his son John, from his mother's keeping and made him a ward of Archbishop Abbot to insure the boy was not raised as a Roman Catholic.

John was educated at Oxford until the King decided he should come to Court. In 1616 when James' son Charles was created Prince of Wales, John was made a Knight Baronet and the unpaid fine of £10,000 which had blighted the family's life since his father's death was remitted.

In 1621, at the age of 18, Elizabeth, who was said to be of a serious almost puritanical disposition, married John Mordaunt at Blechingley Place, the house which she had inherited from her father.

The Mordaunt family seat was at Lowick in Northamptonshire and it was here the couple's first son was born. Named William after his Howard grand-father he was soon followed by Henry, Elizabeth and yet another John, the only three of the couple's children to reach maturity.

Elizabeth grew up to marry Thomas, son and heir of Edward Howard, first Lord Howard of Escrick, thus strengthening family ties with the widespread Howard clan.

But William, who would have become the 2nd Earl of Peterborough, had he lived, sadly, only survived for 82 days and was buried at Lowick leaving Henry to become his father's heir.

John, the youngest , was born at his mother's childhood home in Blechingley on the 18th June 1626 and was baptised two days later.

In the years that followed, their father was to receive further favours from the crown, being created first Earl of Peterborough in 1627/8.

With Henry now his heir, the new Earl and his wife , both well educated themselves, began to consider their son's future education.

They at last settled on Sir Henry Wotton, diplomat, courtier, poet and friend of John Donne, as the most suitable man to oversee their son's life until it was time for him to take his place at court.

Sir Henry was no newcomer to this type of work. On an earlier diplomatic mission to Savoy, he had been accompanied by the future Duke of Newcastle and his brother Charles Cavendish together with several other young nobles. His job being amongst other things to supervise their education and instil in the young gentlemen both good manners and an appreciation of art in Europe, together with an insight into how Englishmen were expected to behave when dealing with foreigners.

And so young Henry was despatched to join him in lodgings at Eton, followed shortly after by his brother John.

However, this peaceful interlude did not last for long. Storm clouds were gathering on the horizon.

Relations between King and Parliament, not good at the best of times, were now at breaking point, but the Countess had other things on her mind. In August 1639 her step-grandmother died and was buried at Chelsea.

Now began the battle between the Mordaunts and Lord Monson, Lady Margaret's widower.

When the Lord Admiral died, he left Reigate Priory to his widow for her lifetime and on her death, the estate was to pass to his grandaughter Elizabeth, as her father, his son, was already dead.

But Lady Margaret remarried and for the 12 years before her death, her new husband, Lord Monson, had treated the estate and its revenues as his own and was therefore loth to give them up.

The Mordaunts were forced to pursue their claims through the courts and although in 1642, Elizabeth managed to secure the Priory, the final claims were not settled until Lord Monson's death in 1671.

By the beginning of 1639/40 it had become clear that war was inevitable. Henry was removed from Eton and sent with his younger brother John to the continent, to finish their education out of harm's way.

When the King raised his standard at Nottingham, the Earl of Peterborough chose to support Parliament and his wife being, of a serious almost Puritan turn of mind, supported him. He received a commission from Parliament as general of the Ordnance under the Earl of Essex and out of his own pocket met the expense of raising a troop to fight the King. Early in 1642 Henry returned from the continent to join his father.

The first Earl of Peterborough's war was not a long one, he died of consumption on the 18th June 1642. Luckily, Elizabeth had by now regained Reigate Priory from Lord Monson, who at one point had placed cannon in the grounds to deter the Countess, threatening to shoot if she tried to gain entrance.

With the reclaiming of the Priory the Countess could have been forgiven if she thought her problems were over, but with the death of her husband her troubles had just begun.

In 1643, Henry, now the 2nd Earl of Peterborough deserted to the King at Oxford. His mother held this as an unpardonable act of treachery to his father's memory and took steps to disinherit him in favour of John, her younger son.

The enmity between them rumbled on long after Charles II's restoration and Elizabeth never really forgave Henry.

Having been wounded in the King's cause Henry spent the later part of the struggle on the continent. He was back in England in the summer of 1647 and had a private interview with the captive King who was being taken to Hampton Court. Early in the following spring both Henry and John were persuaded to join the ill fated and badly organised rising led by Henry Rich, the Earl of Holland with the aim of restoring the King. Doomed to fail from the start the adventure ended with a badly wounded Henry escaping to Antwerp.

He returned to England the following year and again compounded for his estates.

During these years Elizabeth had lived quietly at Reigate, the family fortune had dwindled due to her sons' adherance to the Royalist cause and the long legal battle fought with Lord Monson.

Sometime during 1654/5, she decided to move the magnificently carved oak fire surround from the now dilapidated Blechingley Place and install it in the Priory.

Her friend John Evelyn, the diarist, visiting the Priory in 1655 thought it worth recording the event.

Another visitor to Reigate was Archbishop Usher, who found sanctuary with the Countess in 1646 and stayed until his death on the 20th March 1655/6.

Although in the years leading up to the Restoration Elizabeth was to pay heavily for her son John's delinquency, once Charles II was back on the throne she was again scheming on his behalf.

In 1647 on Henry's last meeting with King Charles I he had felt it necessary to extract a promise from the King concerning his inheritance.
According to a statement dated September 21st 1647 given at Hampton Court;

[4]

> *" Promise by the King to Henry, Earl of Peterborough. That he will withhold his consent to any application by the (Dowager) Countess of Peterborough for cutting off the entail of certain lands (including the Priory of Ryegate), whereto the present Earl is heritable by virtue of an entail of the gift of the Crown and of which the reversion expectant thereof is in his Majesty".*

The moment Charles II was safely on the throne Henry once more laid claim to his rights. A statement of the case reads .....

[5]

> *"....the present Countess Dowager obtained of his Majesty (Charles II) by suprise a grant of the remander of a great part of Ryegate Priory, whereby it became in her power solely to dispose of and alienate that part of it, valued at £800 per annum, which accordingly she did, giving it to her younger son Lord Mordaunt. She further yet endevours to obtain the like grace from his Majesty of the remainder of the rest of that Priory, not withstanding the late King by his warrant declared that this should never be done."*

A footnote attempted to put the King
in the picture

6

> *"To this his Majesty may please to consider*
> *that the only reason of the Mothers secret*
> *aversion to her eldest son arises from his*
> *having so early engaged himself in his*
> *late Majesty's service at Oxford."*

After 29 years of widowhood Elizabeth died in
November 1671, and was buried at Chelsea on the
18th of November 1671.

But, even before she was settled in her grave, Henry
and John were quarrelling over the ownership of the
Priory. Expensive litigation followed and the affair
was finally settled with a compromise.

John kept the Priory whilst Henry received what
was left of the Blechingley estate.

Sources

1.   Parish Registers, Chelsea.
2.   Parich Registers, Reigate.
3.   Parish Registers, Chelsea.
4.   Calendar of State Papers. Domestic.
5.   Calendar of State Papers. Domestic.
6.   Calendar of State Papers. Domestic.

The Turncoat

Reigate Castle from an engraving dated 1785 showing the remaining single storey building and ruined walls, much as they would have looked to the Earl of Holland in June 1648.

Author's Notes

The **George Villiers** mentioned in this
chapter is the second Duke of Buckingham,
not to be confused with his father, **Charles I's**
favourite, who was stabbed to death by a
dissatisfied soldier called **Felton** at
Portsmouth in August 1628.
George, the son, was raised at the Court
of Charles I and was involved with the
disastrous events of the second civil war.
He married **Sir Thomas Fairfax's** daughter
Mary and after the Restoration turned his
hand to writing plays one of which, 'The
Rehearsal' was said to be the prototype
for **Sheridan's** 'The Critic'. Totally without
principles he never fulfilled his early promise,
he quarrelled with Charles II and almost every
one else at Court. His constitution was unable
to keep up with his life style and he retired to
the country to live, broken both in health and
fortune. He died in 1687, after catching a chill
whilst digging out a fox from its den.

You could not have found a more unsuitable person than Henry Rich, Earl of Holland to lead a clandestine rising against Parliament.

According to a Royalist pamphlet written in 1648 just after the event;

> "...he shifted his parties as often as his
> mother did her husbands, and yet plaid
> loose with both..." [1]

In 1642 he was supporting the Parliamentarian cause and at Turnham Green acting as Field Marshal of the day under the Earl of Essex.

The next year he became one of the leaders of the Peace Party and tried to persuade Essex to back him with the might of his army. When this plan failed, Holland went over to the King and was with Charles at the siege of Gloucester. He took part in the first battle of Newbury, serving with the King's Own Regiment of horse, but when he did not receive the promotion he thought his due he changed sides once again.

When the House of Lords had him arrested he managed to persuade them that with his defection to the King, he had the country's interests at heart and that his plan was to promote peace between Charles and Parliament. However, the Catholic faction at Court had proved too strong and thwarted his noble intentions so he had returned to his true allegiance.

In 1645 he petitioned for compensation for losses incurred in his support for Parliament during the war. He complained that he had lost approximately £10,000 in pensions and salaries from various offices, not to mention the £30,000 owed him by the King, which he was never likely to see again.

The House of Commons was not convinced that the claim was justified and even withdrew the offer of £1000 a year pension that the Lords had considered offering him.

Finding no friends in the Parliamentarian camp Holland again changed his coat. This time, attempting to mediate between the English Presbyterian leaders and the Scottish Commissioners. When this failed and with the outset of the second civil war he obtained a General's commission from the Prince of Wales, later Charles II. Holland then set about plotting with the Earl of Lauderdale to free the King.

On the 23rd May 1648 a 'rising' broke out in Kent which was to culminate in a decisive defeat for the King's supporters at Maidstone. Those lucky enough to escape across the river fled to the Royalist held castle at Colchester, hotly pursued by Parliamentary troops under Thomas Fairfax.

With the Lord General's attention centred on Colchester, Holland took the opportunity to put in motion events which were intended to precipitate a popular rising in Surrey and Sussex. He persuaded a group of young Royalist gentlemen to join him in his enterprise which he assured everyone willing to listen was to restore the King to his throne and bring peace to the nation.

He was financed by Lady Carlisle who pawned her necklace to provide him with funds, but the whole affair was so mismanaged to the disgust of his own troops that after the event one of them published his own account of the fiasco entitle of "The Decoy"

> ".. . being principally assisted therein by
> that English Jezabel, The Countess of
> Carlisle, and perswades them, who had
> money and means to advance his Majesties
> cause, to engage all they could to arme with
> them...." [2]

With Fairfax at Colchester and Cromwell in Wales the Earl sent a letter to the Aldermen of the City of London announcing his intentions;

> " ...to release and preserve his Majesty's
> person, to bring him to his Parliament, to
> settle Peace in the Kingdom, and to preserve
> the known laws..." [3]

and

> "... inviting the City to joyn with them herein,
> at least not to be active against them..." [4]

He then appeared at Kingston, accompanied by the Duke of Buckingham, his brother Lord Francis Villiers, the Earl of Peterborough and his brother, John Mordaunt, together with a Dutch or German mercenary, a one time quartermaster to the Army of Parliament, Colonel Dalbeer. Their forces numbered between 500 and 600 troops both horse and foot.

The night before joining Holland at Kingston, Lord Francis had spent with his mistress, Mary Kirke. In anticipation that he might not return from so hazardous an adventure, he gave her a present of plate worth £1000. She in return gave him a lock of her hair, sown into a ribbon which he wore next to his heart.

On the 6th July the Royalist force marched out of Kingston for Reigate where they intended to garrison the castle. Travelling via Leatherhead and Dorking they hoped to pick up more support on the way.

On their arrival at Reigate the Royalists began looting not only the supporters of Parliament but those who supported the King as well, even shooting one resident who refused to hand over his pistols.
The popular support that Holland had counted on, was not forthcoming.

Meanwhile, the Derby House Committee had ordered a Captain Pretty with a troop of Ireton's horse to go to Kingston and arrest the conspirators.
He arrived shortly after Holland had left and proceeded to capture 17 stragglers whom he conveyed prisoner to Windsor.

The Committee also requested General Fairfax to release a regiment of horse, then besieging Colchester, to protect the City and put down the insurrection.

Fairfax declined the request and instead a message was sent to the commander of the Kentish forces, Sir Michael Livesey, who was, in any case, nearer to Reigate, being at Sevenoaks, with several troops of horse.

On receiving the order Livesey sent his deputy, Major Gibbons and several troops of horse to Reigate while he followed more slowly with the rest of the horse and foot.

At the same time, Major Lewis Audeley, a Surrey man by marriage, his wife being the widow of Ralph Hawtry of Sanderstead, was at Hounslow with a further 3 troops of Livesey's Horse. He was also ordered to follow Holland and report back. Being told there was to be a rendezvous of Royalists on Banstead Downs, under cover of a horse race, he went there first, but, as there was no sign of any meeting, he rode towards Reigate , taking a course parallel to the Royalists but slightly to the north. On reaching Red Hill, he drew up his small force and wheeled around to face the Cavaliers, his rear protected by the advancing Gibbons and Livesey.

Finding Holland had placed sentries on Red Hill Common in the area of White Post Hill a sharp exchange ensued and Audeley beat off the Royalist guard who retreated to Reigate.

Unsure of the enemy's strength, Audeley wisely decided to camp for the night and await the forces from Kent under Major Gibbons.

The arrival of the Parliamentarian Horse had caused consternation in the Royalist camp and Holland decided discretion was the better part of valour and marched his troops back the way they had come to Dorking.

Major Gibbons, coming post haste from Sevenoaks missed Audeley and rode straight to Reigate where he found neither friend nor foe. He also withdrew, joining forces with Audeley at first light, on the 7th July. After a hasty conference they decided rather than pursue a force whose strength they were unsure of, they would wait for Sir Michael to arrive with reinforcements.

At the same time Holland, who had been informed, wrongly as it turned out, that Reigate was empty of enemy forces, decided to march forth once more and occupy the castle.

Alas for the Royalists, on reaching Reigate they found both Audeley and Gibbons occupying the town and in confusion turned tail for Kingston.

About two hours after this, the main body of Parliamentary troops arrived, a force made up of 5 troops of horse and 3 of foot from Livesey's regiment, 2 troops of Major Riches and Major Gibbons' own troop, with Sir Michael at their head.

Leaving a garrison of some 20 men under the command of Mr. Fenneck in the castle, Livesey marched forth in pursuit of the departed Royalists, who he harrassed all the way towards Ewell.

At last the Royalists turned to face them but Sir Michael was reluctant to engage until all his troops had caught up.

By way of a prelude each side sent out a number of men who fought in single combat, men who according to Audeley;

"....played valiently...." [5]

With both sides reluctant to commit their entire forces Sir Michael's troops continued to harrass the Royalists until they reached Surbiton where a sharper skirmish ensued.

Low moral and the disorganised nature of the Royalist chain of command may to some extent explain their unwillingness to fight. They lacked even the basic necessities for an army, being woefully short of powder and shot and even the weapons to use it in. Horses were scarce, there was no money for food for either men or animals. Holland had gone off so half-cocked that the enterprise was doomed from the start.

According to an eyewitness:

6

> " ...some in the Head of Colonell Leggs
> Troop, seeing a partie whom before they
> had not noted, gave word face about,
> whereupon ensued such a rout, that divers
> quitted their horses, the foot their armes,
> our wagons were overthrowne, drivers
> betook themselves unto the adjoyning
> woods......being redeemed from the
> inconveniences this mistake put us into,
> and rallied again we marched.....

Lord Francis Villiers was one of the few casualties
sustained by either force. He had his horse killed under him
and continued to fight on foot, spurning offers of quarter,
until tiring at last he was killed by a trooper who managed
to get behind him and knocked off his helmet.   As the
running fight neared Kingston Bridge the Royalist
cavalry were met by their foot:

7

> "...their horse suddenly shewed themselves
> for their best advantage, advancing towards
> us , upon which some amongst us cryed out,
> the Armie, the Armie, we are all betrayed, no
> stop could be made of our running, untill we
> came unto Kingstone.......where we met
> with our foot who cryed shame at us, and
> threatened to fire upon us, in Kingstone it
> was often propounded that we should rallie,
> but never effected, yea after the Bridge was
> stopped by our ownWaggon, the horse drew
> over in a file, and then for the greater part
> every man shifted for himselfe."

Livesey took a number of prisoners and horse, but not knowing the enemy's exact strength he refrained from entering Kingston until the morning when he found all the Royalists fled. He was able to seize without opposition some hundred horses and their carriages which had been left behind in the flight.

The Royalist leaders and their few remaining horse headed north but were intercepted at St. Neots on July 10th by Scrope's regiment sent from Colchester. Dalbeer was killed and Holland surrendered whilst Buckingham and Peterborough fled abroad. John Mordaunt, after lying low for sometime, returned to Reigate and compounded his estates.

Parliament, believing Francis Villiers to be alive but wounded, sent a surgeon with a message that he was to be treated with all courtesy. But the unfortunate Francis was already dead. His body was rowed down the Thames from Kingston to York House and taken up through the watergate built by Inigo Jones for his father, to be buried in the Henry VII chapel at Westminster Abbey.

At his trial for treason Holland claimed he was no part of the plot but had come on the rebels by chance and been unable to win free. In view of his past behaviour and despite the efforts of his relatives and the few friends that remained to him he was found guilty and executed with the Duke of Hamilton and Lord Capel who was captured at the siege of Colchester, on the 9th March, 1648/9.

N

Hounslow

Kingston upon Thames

Ewell

Banstead Downs

Dorking

Reigate

Red Hill Common

Westerham

Sevenoaks

The Earl of Holland's route on 6th and 7th July 1648 × × × ×
Major Audeley's march 6th July 1648 . . . .
Route taken by the combined Parliamentary forces — · — · —

45

Sources

1. The Decoy,1648.
2. The Decoy,1648.
3. Bulstrode Whitelocke - Memorials of
    English Affairs.
4. Bulstrode Whitelocke - Memorials of
    English Affairs.
5. Major Lewis Audeley - A true relation.. 1648.
    Ref. E. 451. (30) British Library.
6. The Decoy, 1648
7. The Decoy, 1648.
    Ref. R3 4206, Kingston-upon-Thames, Library.

The Saint and the Roundhead.

17th century Merchant ship of the type used
by Colonists travelling to the New World.

Author's Notes

For those not familiar with the numerous factions that sprang up during the CivilWars. **The Levellers** were a democratic movement who demanded greater social reforms and basically believed all men were created equal. The **Fifth Monarchy Men** believed that the Kingdom of God was at hand and that the Fourth Monarchy, that of Rome was about to be overthrown and that the Fifth, the reign of King Jesus would then begin as prophesied in the **Book of Daniel,** when all men who believed would be known as **Saints.**

During the summer of 1647, with Charles I in the hands of the Army, many people considered the war was as good as over.

Unfortunately, Parliament decided it no longer needed an Army of such strength, and took steps to disband those Regiments not needed for service in Ireland. However, they neglected to settle the arrears of pay, which, in the case of the Infantry was at least 18 weeks and the Cavalry some 43. Fairfax and Cromwell set up a "General Council of the Army", with representatives from each Regiment, to treat with Parliament. During these exchanges, numerous troops were billeted in the countryside around London . Among these were men of Captain Dury's Company, who were quartered in Reigate, much to the dismay of the locals.

In August 1647 these soldiers were attacked by an enemy far deadlier than they had faced in any earlier engagement.

The Plague had come to Reigate !

Within days a number of soldiers had succumbed and were buried according to Parish records in St. Mary's churchyard.

Throughout that summer and into autumn the plague raged and people continued to die.

In November a further 28 of Captain Dury's troopers died, but with the coming of the colder weather, the plague itself died down.

Winter turned the roads to quagmires, making travel almost impossible. For those soldiers enjoying "Free Quarter" in the hostile environment of Reigate, it brought an unwelcome idleness and as the saying goes "The Devil makes work for idle hands".

One Tuesday in February 1647/8, trouble broke out at the weekly market. Exactly what or who started the affray we may never know. Perhaps some townsman, well in his cups, made a scathing comment about the soldiery, it may be a soldier made a remark about the King and after months of ill feeling this was the straw that broke the camel's back. What ever the cause, fighting broke out and by the end of the day, two local men lay dead. Those who died were Nicholas Marden and 24 year old William Preist of Nutfield.

The entry for 22nd February 1647/8 in St. Mary's register reads..

[1]

> " Ni. Marden and William Preist both
> wounded the Tuesday before..... by
> some of the souldiers of Capt.
> Winthorps Troope in Coll. Harrison's
> Regiment in Sir Thos. Fairfax Armie,
> being quartered in the Town fell out
> withe the Country men and these two,
> murdered by them and many more
> dangerously wounded. "

Those of you who have read Hooper's **Reigate through the Ages,** will no doubt be familiar with these tragic events, but the officer in charge, Captain Winthorp, was in fact Stephen Winthrop, the 4th son of John Winthrop, one time Governor of the Massachusetts Bay Company, and his 3rd wife, Margaret Tyndall.

Stephen was born at Groton in Suffolk, on the 24th March 1618/9 and spent the first years of his life at Groton Manor, the family home.

But, in 1629 when he was just 10 years old, events took place which were to change his life.

The religious climate of England, especially for those of the Puritan faith was becoming intolerable.

In May 1629 came the first intimation that John Winthrop was considering leaving England. He wrote to his wife Margaret...

[2]

> *My dear wife,*
> *I am verylye persuaded God will bring some heavye affliction upon this lande, and that speedylye.... if the Lord seeth it will be good for us, he will provide a shelter and a hiding-place for us and others, as a Zoar for Lott...."*.

With the dissolution of Parliament in 1629 he lost his post. This and the death of his mother may have finally persuaded him to seek a better life for himself and his family in the New world.

On the 22 March 1629/30, John Winthrop and two of his children set sail from Southampton, on the 'Arbella'. Margaret was forced to delay her own departure for nearly a year as she was pregnant.

The 'Arbella' was also delayed; contrary winds kept them anchored off the Isle of Wight for nearly a fortnight before they were eventually able to set sail for America. But with *"Gods help and protection"* after a voyage of some sixty six days the ship made anchor in Salem harbour on the 17th June 1630.

From their landing until his death in March 1648/9 John Winthrop was considered a man of good standing in the colony, he was elected Governor of the Massachusetts Bay Company on numerous occasions.

A letter sent to Secretary Coke in 1632 describes him as...

".....a discreet and sober man, wearing plain apparel, assisting in any ordinary labour, and ruling with much mildness and justice." [3]

With the outbreak of Civil War the Colonists in the main had managed to keep themselves apart, but by the end of 1645, having seen the political situation worsening by the day, John Winthrop's sons decided that their duty lay with the Army of Parliament in England.

On his return, Stephen, who was married to Judith, the daughter of Captain William Rainsborough, was invited by his brother-in-law, also William, to join Sheffield's Regiment of Horse, in the New Model Army. At this time the regiment's Colonel was Thomas, one of the many sons of Edmund, Lord Sheffield, first Earl of Mulgrave and in April 1646 they took part in the siege of Barnstaple in Devon. It was to Colonel Sheffield that Sir Thomas Fairfax gave the duty of overseeing the Royalist's surrender. However, despite sterling service, in 1647 Parliament decided to disband them. Colonel Sheffield undertook to try to persuade his soldiers to take service in Ireland. But his troops wanted nothing to do with this unpopular posting unless Parliament first settled their arrears of pay.

By the end of May 1647, they were reported to be on the verge of mutiny and at the beginning of June, Sheffield left the regiment.

A new colonel was appointed by Fairfax in the person of Thomas Harrison, a Fifth Monarchy man.

Harrison was in charge of the Regiment at the time of the unfortunate incident at Reigate

With the arrival of the new Colonel, William Rainsborough was promoted to major, while Stephen Winthrop took over the troop formerly commanded by Captain Robert Robottom.

After some months of inactivity while Parliament and the Army argued over their allegiance, the Regiment was dispatched to Cheshire to oppose Sir Marmaduke Langdale and his Cavaliers.

Fairfax wrote to the Derby House Committee in May 1648...

> *"I am now sending Col. Harrison with his*[4] *regiment of horse, and some others, into Cheshire to oppose their further proceedings, and, with what assistance he can get from the gentry and well affected in those parts, to endeavour the clearing of them from the adverse forces."*

On their arrival Sir Marmaduke retreated, leaving Harrison and his regiment to join forces with Major-General Lambert in Cumberland.

In early July 1648 they were ordered to ride north to deal with a large party of Scots under the Duke of Hamilton. Outnumbered by Hamilton's forces, Harrison and Lambert were forced to retreat and at Appleby on Monday 17th July, the now General Harriso received a wound which could have proved fatal.

He was dispatched to Lancaster to seek treatment, but his regiment, including Stephen Winthrop, marched towards Preston, were on the 17th August, they met with the Scots' army.

By nightfall 4,000 of Hamilton's men were taken prisoner and over 1000 slain. The remnant of the Scots' forces were pursued back over the border and it was not until the end of October that the Regiment again marched south.

In December, the now recovered Harrison was placed in command of the guard which brought King Charles from Hurst Castle to Windsor.

He was accompanied by one troop of his regiment whilst the rest of his men were kept in the Midlands.

All through December the Army continued to try and negotiate a settlement with the King, but on Christmas Day 1648 the talks broke down for the final time owing to Charles' intransigence.

From then on, events went forward with frightening speed. On the 6th January 1648/9 a "High Court of Justice" was convened to try the King on a charge of treason. The verdict was never in doubt. The King was found guilty and sentenced to death. He was executed outside the Banqueting Hall at Whitehall on the 30th January.

Less than three months later Stephen Winthrop was to receive news of the death of his father, who died on the 26th of March 1648/9. He was survived by his fourth wife Martha, who he had married early in 1648 after the death of Margaret on 14th of June 1647.

At the time of their marriage Martha was the widow of Thomas Cotymore, who brought with her a substantial estate. Which was just as well, as her new husband had lost most of his money due to the dishonesty of his bailiff. Martha was also the daughter of Captain William Rainsborough and sister to Stephen's wife Judith.

This made John his daughter-in-law's father-in-law and brother-in-law at the same time, whilst Stephen was his father's son and brother-in-law. A genealogist's nightmare !

John Winthrop was buried in the King's Chapel graveyard, on the 3rd April, with a funeral salute fired by the Honourable Artillery Company of Boston.

In England the death of the King did not bring the desired peace.

By May 1649 parts of the Army were in open revolt. The mutiny, instigated by the Levellers, had its roots in the old problems of arrears in pay and the dislike of fighting abroad.

Parliament had decided to send an army of 12,000 men under the command of Cromwell to reconquer Ireland. Four cavalry regiments were chosen, Scroope's; Ireton's; Horton's and Lambert's. No soldier was obliged to go, if he prefered, he could take his discharge but, if he did, he was prohibited from re-enlisting in any other regiment.

The soldier's main complaint was that, if they accepted their discharge, they were not being paid enough of their arrears even to get to their homes, let alone set themselves up to earn a living when they got there.

Fairfax tried to persuade them they would receive all the arrears in time but Scroope's regiment would have none of it.

Their Commander and a few of his officers joined Fairfax at his headquarters near Alton in Hampshire, the rest of the Regiment marched off towards Old Sarum.

Here they were joined by member of Ireton's Horse and the mutineers then rode in the direction of Wantage. Here they hoped to rendezvous with Harrison's regiment, but Fairfax had left Andover with the intention of stopping them.

When the mutineers reached Blagrove they were disappointed to find only two troops from Harrison's regiment waiting for them, those of Captains Peck and Winthrop.

The rest of the regiment stayed loyal to the Army, perhaps due to their Colonel's presence and neither Peck nor Winthrop were blamed for their soldiers' disobedience. But Fairfax and Cromwell followed the twelve troops of mutineers to Burford. There, on the night of the 14th May they attacked. By morning they had captured a number of prisoners together with the arms and horses of over 800 men.

A Council of War was convened and four of the ringleaders were tried and sentenced to death.

James Thompson, Corporal Perkins and John Church were shot in Burford churchyard while Cornet Den was reprieved at the eleventh hour.

Scroope's regiment was completely disbanded, although their Colonel became Governor of Bristol Castle from October 1649 to 1655, even though his active military career was more or less finished. At the Restoration he was tried as a Regicide and executed on the 17th October 1660.

".... a comely ancient gentleman...." [5]

According to a pamphlet printed at the time.

One other casualty of Burford was Major Rainsborough. Cromwell considered his influence bad for discipline and had him dismissed from the Army. The rest of the regiment were moved to Wales and on the 21st of August 1649, Harrison was appointed Commander-in-Chief of all forces in Monmouth, Hereford, South Wales and all Gloucestershire, west of the Severn.

On the 14th July 1650, Stephen Winthrop was writing -

" I am in Wales, and am left with some [6]
horrsse to keep quiett these parts."

Stephen, who had been promoted to Major was zealous in his efforts *" to keepe quiete these partts "*, in August that year, acting on information received, he arrested Colonel Edward Harley, who had been an officer in Colonel Pride's regiment, on the grounds that he was...

"... disaffected to the government." [7]

It was this Colonel Pride of 'Pride's Purge' fame who once represented Reigate in Parliament.

When in the Summer of 1650 war with Scotland broke out, Harrison was appointed Commander-in-Chief of the forces then in the south of England, during the absence of Cromwell. This position did not last very long as by March 1651, Cromwell had ordered him north, with the job of recruiting more forces to face the Scots' threat. By July the Regiment was in Edinburgh, but when in early August, Charles II embarked on his ill fated march towards Worcester, Harrison was hot on his heels with 3,000 horse.

Charles occupied the city of Worcester and when, on the 3rd of September, battle commenced, Major General Harrison's brigade fought to the east of the river Severn.

The Royalist force of some 12,000 men was heavily outnumbered, Cromwell having between 25,000 and 30,000 horse and foot.

The King watched the battle from the tower of Worcester Cathedral until, believing that Cromwell had overstretched his forces, he gathered his cavalry and all the available infantry and sallied out of the Sudbury Gate to face Cromwell's right wing. After some three hours hard fighting, just as it looked as if Charles would be successful, Cromwell pushed forward reinforcements of regular cavalry. The Royalist Horse broke and were pursued through the narrow streets of Worcester, escaping by the North Gate. But for the infantry there was no escape and as night fell, they surrendered in droves.

Between 6,000 and 7, 000 prisoners were taken on the site of the battle and those that escaped the city were ruthlessly hunted down. Charles himself spent many days wandering back and forth across the south of England, until he was at last able to find a shipmaster willing to risk taking him to France.

After Worcester, Harrison's star was in the ascendance, he was second only to Cromwell in the Army .

When Cromwell decided to put an end to the sitting of Parliament, it was Harrison at his side who persuaded the Speaker to quit his seat.

But, with Cromwell established as Protector, Harrison's military and political career came to an end. He declined to take orders from the new Lord Protector and on the 21st December 1653, his commission was withdrawn.

In the following February he was ordered home
to his estate in Staffordshire, but refused to go. He was
then sent in custody to Herefordshire and spent the next
few months there, under surveillance.

From February 1654/55 to March 1656 he was
held in close confinement, first at Portsmouth and then,
like Charles I, at Carisbrooke on the Isle of Wight.
Over the next few years he was constantly in trouble.
Trouble that was nearly always connected with the plots
of his fellow Fifth Monarchy Men.

On the eve of the Restoration he ignored his friends'
urging to leave the country and in April 1660, was arrested
at his home in Staffordshire. Taken to the Tower, he was
tried at the Old Bailey on the 10th of October and pleaded

"not guilty." [8]

He admitted he had signed the King's death
warrant, but justified it by saying...

> *"I did what I did, as out of conscience* [9]
> *to the Lord"*

adding

> *"May be I might be a little mistaken; but I* [10]
> *did it all according to the best of my*
> *understanding, desiring to make the*
> *revealed will of God in his Holy*
> *Scriptures as a guide to me."*

The verdict was a foregone conclusion.
Harrison was executed on the 13th October 1660.

Pepys who witnessed the event described him as ...

[11]

*"....looking as cheerful as any man could
in that condition...*

He died with great courage and his last words
to the watching crowd were...

[12]

*"By God I have leapt over a wall, by
God I have run through a troop,
and by God I will go through this
death, and he will make it easy for me."*

He was hung, drawn and quartered and his head
was set on a pole on the south east end of Westminster
Hall, looking towards London . His body is said to be
buried in St. Giles' churchyard, Newcastle-under-Lyme,
but the gravestone has now vanished.

[13]

*" So went the earthly Saint to join the
Company of the Celestial."*

Stephen Winthrop fought at Worcester but his
health was failing fast.

On the 13th June 1651 a son, called Stephen after
his father , was born to Judith at Groton and in 1652
in expectation of leaving the Army, Stephen bought a
house and part of Marylebone Park for his family.
It was there his daughters Judith and Margaret were born.

Then in January 1653/54 the remnants of
Harrison's regiment were sent to Scotland to suppress
a rising led by the Earl of Glencairn.

The Commander-in-chief in Scotland, Colonel Lilburne wrote to the Protector on the 21st of February asking for...

> [14]
> "...some officers to take care of Major General Harrison's regiment, the major (Winthrop) being weake, and never a Captain to assist him."

In May that year General Monck reported...

> [15]
> "Major-General Harrison's major being ill, and unfit to endure the field, I have given him liberty to goe for England, and I thincke hee will hardly return againe."

It was reported abroad that Henry Cromwell was to be the Regiment's new Colonel but his father sent him to Ireland instead and Stephen Winthrop was appointed in his place.

He had been ill for many months and on the 2nd of August 1653, wrote to his brother John....

> [16]
> "I have noe health heare, amd I have beene this two years extreamly troubled with the zeatica, and am just now going to the Bath to see if that may remedy it. My much lying in wet fields upon the ground hath brought it vppon me, as it hath vppon many others. It makes my life very uncomfortable."

He told John how much he would like to
return to America, if he were well enough. By 1656
his health must have improved as he represented
Banff and Aberdeen in the assembly of 1656.
But by winter that year he was once more ill and
writes of having to keep to his chamber through
out the winter.

"I have not my health longe togither heer",[17]

and then adds

*"eyre is two moist for me, and breeds
rumes and coughes."*

He never recovered his health and in 1658, after

"laying verry sick."[18]

he died, leaving behind a widow and young family.

Sources

1. Parish Registers, Reigate.
2. R.C. Winthrop - Life & letters of John Winthrop Vols. One and Two 1864-7. Cambridge 1887.
3. Calandar of State Papers - Colonial 1574-1660.
4. Calandar of State Papers - Domestic
5. British Library.
6. Massachusetts Historical Society - Collections.
7 Portland Mss. Public Records Office.
8. State Trials. Library of Houses of Parliament
9. State Trials.   "   "   "
10. State Trials.   "   "   "
11. Samuel Pepys' diary.
12. Proceedings of the American Antiquarian Society.
13. British Library.
14. Firth & Davies - Regimental History of Cromwell's Army OUP 1939
15. Firth - Scotland and the Protectorate OUP 1899
16. Massachusetts Historical Society.
17. Massachusetts Historical Society.
18. Massachusetts Historical Society.
19. Massachusetts Historical Society,
    1154, Boylston Street,
    Boston,
    Massachusetts, MA 02215
    USA

The Royalist

Copyright of Surrey History Service

John Mordaunt 1627-1675

Author's Notes

Regarding the quotes from the Diaries of
Pepys and **John Evelyn.** Numerous copies
of both of these works have been published
over the years since they first went to press.
I have therefore refrained from mentioning
any one particular edition leaving the Reader,
should they wish to follow it up, a wider
choice.

John Mordaunt was born at Blechingley in 1627.

He was the third son of John Mordaunt, first Earl of Peterborough and his wife Elizabeth, grand-daughter and heiress of Charles Howard of Effingham, the Lord Admiral.

His early childhood was spent between his father's family home, at Drayton House, near Lowick in Northamptonshire, Arundell House, in London, the Howard's town house and Blechingley Place, the house his mother had inherited on the death of her father, William.

At the outbreak of Civil War, the 13 year old John was sent with his elder brother, Henry, to the continent to continue his education, out of harm's way. When Henry returned to England in 1642, John stayed on, travelling widely in both France and Italy. In 1648 Henry became involved with Henry Rich, the Earl of Holland, in his attempt to free the King, and John, then just 21, hastened home to join them.

Unfortunately for the Royalists concerned, the plot was a dismal failure. After an abortive attempt to raise support in the home counties, the Earl was captured and later executed. Henry escaped to Antwerp, and although badly wounded he survived, but was forced to spend a number of years living in exile in both France and Holland.

John went into hiding for some months, but when the heat died down, he emerged to make his peace with Parliament.

Although ostensibly living a quiet life with his widowed mother at Reigate Priory, he continued to plot for the restoration of the Stuart monarchy.

During the early 1650's he met and courted a distant relative of his mother's, Elizabeth, the second daughter of Thomas Carey, who was the youngest son of Robert Carey, first Earl of Monmouth.

This lady was, according to Clarendon,

[1]

> *"...a young and beautiful lady; of a very loyal spirit and notable vivacity of will and humour, who concured with him in all honourable dedication of himself."*

She became a special favourite of John Evelyn, who visited her often, both at the Priory and in London, mentioning her in his diaries on numerous occasions.

However, married life proved no bed of roses, Elizabeth's patience must have been sorely tried by her husband's continual plotting. Less than a year after their marriage, he re-commenced corresponding with the earl of Ormonde, with a view to restoring the monarchy, but their plots came to nought.

In 1657, Charles II secretly sent John a commission to raise troops for a Royalist rising in Sussex. Unfortunately, the letters fell into the hands of John Thurloe, Cromwell's Spy Master and in April 1658 John Mordaunt was arrested and sent to the Tower.

Mordaunt's trial took place in the Painted Chamber at Westminster, on the 2nd of June, when in the company of Dr. John Hart and Sir Henry Slingsby, he was arranged on a charge of high treason.

The Court was comprised of forty members of Parliament acting as both judge and jury, with Lord-Commissioner Lisle as its president.

At first John disputed the court's validity, giving his wife and mother time to approach those jurymen who they thought might be persuaded of his innocence.

The Dowager Lady Peterborough was highly respected and according to Evelyn , John's wife was...

"...the most virtuous Lady in the world..." [2]

This did not stop the two ladies who, acting on some friendly advice, arranged for one of the key witnesses for the prosecution, to take a visit to the country, and to distribute such largesse as they could raise, among the well affected members of the jury. When this was done the young Lady Mordaunt managed to get a message to her husband begging him..

" For God's sake plead, plead for my sake, and stand disputing no longer !" [3]

Pleading *"Not Guilty"* , he managed to discredit some of the evidence against him.

At that point, Colonel Pride, who had been MP for Reigate, was taken ill and withdrew from the proceedings. Of the remaining 38 members, 19 voted for acquittal and 19 condemned Mordaunt. It was left to Lord Commissioner Lisle to use his casting vote in John's favour.

Evelyn notes...

" I went to visit my Lady Peterborough, whose son, Mr. Mordaunt, a prisoner in the Tower, and was now on his trial, and acquitted by but one vote". [4]

69

No sooner was he free, than John began plotting again. In anticipation of his success, Charles II raised him to the peerage as Baron Mordaunt of Reigate and Viscount Avalon.

As had happened with previous risings, John Thurloe, the Spy Master, was aware of events almost before the participants.

General Fleetwood sent Major Lewis Audeley, who had been involved in putting down the Earl of Holland's rising, to Red Hill Common to arrest any Royalists he should find loitering there. There were but few, who quickly dispersed. With no popular support, John Mordaunt, deemed 'discretion the better part of valour' and went to ground in London before slipping aboard a friendly ship bound for France where he took lodgings in Calais.

In March 1659/60 he left France to join the King in Brussels, but by April 1660, he had returned to England with a letter from Charles to the Mayor and Corporation of London.

When the King landed at Dover on the 25th May 1660 he was met at Barham Down by the ever loyal Mordaunt, ready to escort him back to his capital.

With the King's return his loyal followers looked to him for some recompense for their sufferings, a few, like Mordaunt were lucky, the majority were not. He was made Lord Lieutenant of Surrey and Constable of Windsor Castle, the latter office he held until 1667.

But Mordaunt had made many enemies at court, according to Clarendon, who was one of his supporters:

5

"He was the butt at which all their arrows
of envy, malice and jealousy were aimed
and shot, he was the object and subject
of all their scurrilous jests and depraving
discources and relations...."

The year 1666/7 turned out to be an *"Annus Horribilis"* for Viscount Mordaunt.

In December 1666, a Mr. William Tayleur, who held several "Offices of Trust" at Windsor Castle, petitioned the House of Commons for redress against the actions of his Lordship, whilst he was governor there.

According to the Articles of Impeachment, Mr. Tayleur had in 1660, decided to stand for election as a burgess of the town. Viscount Mordaunt, for reasons of his own, took against him and to prevent his election, on or about the 17th March...

" ...did by soldiers, forcibly eject the said
Mr. Tayleur, together with his wife (then
great with child), family, and goods, out of
the said lodgings and castle, the rude carriage
of which soldiers then frightened a young
child of the said Mr. Tayleur, out of its wits,
whereof it soon died".

From then on things only got worse for the Tayleurs. Mr Tayleur was arrested for debt. Then Viscount Mordaunt ordered him to be taken from the town prison and had him thrown in an underground cell within the precincts of the castle, refusing to accept all offers of bail.

Mr. Tayleur was released the next day but not until after Viscount Mordaunt had threatened to....

[7]

> *"...dispose of the said Mr. Tayleur's places break the Great Seal and justify it when he had done"*

Viscount Mordaunt denied these charges, saying that....

[8]

> *" ... the soldiers assisted the Tayleur family in the removale of their goods and furniture with all civility and as to that the dead child, his lordship cannot think the sight of soldiers should have such effect, the child having been seen playing and well after that time of removal, and as his lordship is informed, was sick of the worms".*

A further charge against John Mordaunt threatened an even bigger scandal. It would appear that he had taken a fancy to Mr. Tayleur's daughter Anne and had been foolish enough to put it in writing.

The impeachment states that...

[9]

> *"....the said Lord Mordaunt in March 1664 did by letters and otherwise, make sundry uncivil addresses to the daughter of William Tayleur, which she rejecting, and threatening to make the said viscount's lady acquainted with them, the said viscount swore by a most dreadful oath and implication, he would persecute her and her family to all eternity".*

Or as Mr. Seymour, one of those appointed to deal with the impeachment said,

> "... here is an illegal dispossession and arbitary imprisonment of William Tayleur, esq., by the Lord accused, because Mr. Tayleur's daughter would not prostitute herself to his lust". [10]

With an eye for a good story the Commons blamed all the events of the 6 years from 1660 on the wicked Lord's desire to have his evil way with the virtuous Miss Tayleur, who would have none of him.

The Common's saw it as a good chance to bring down the House of Lords a peg or two.

Their rather narrow view of the affair does not seem to have gone down very well with their Lordships, the Viscount claiming Mr. Tayleur was guilty of misappropriation and fraud".

With both the Commons and the Lords mindful of their own standing and privileges, the task of how the trial should be conducted was never going to be an easy one to settle.

In January , the Commons requested the Lords appoint a day for the proceedings to begin, but on 26th January, with members of the Commons coming to the bar to present their evidence, a disagreement arose as to the precedent for the impeachment of a Peer of the Realm by them and the meeting was adjourned.

Throughout the rest of the year, messengers went back and forth between the two Houses, with each trying to assert their privileges, until in February 1666/7 the King, himself came to the House of Lords and proroged the Parliament.

Mordaunt was forced to resign his office, but received a full pardon from the King, for all past transgressions, which seems just as well, for according to Pepys, writting on the 29th July, 1667...

[11]

".... above all I saw my Lord Mordaunt as merry as the best, that it seems hath done such further indignities to Mr. Tayleur, since the last sitting of Parliament, as would hang him, if there were nothing else, would the King do what were fit for him, but nothing of that is now likely to be..."

John Mordaunt continued his life at the King's court with no apparent long term damage to his reputation

In 1671, his mother, the Dowager Countess of Peterborough died and he was again in court.

This time the dispute was with his brother Henry over the Reigate estate and after lengthy and acrimonious litigation it ended in compromise.

Mordaunt died on the 5th June 1675, at his home at Parson's Green. Aged just 48, he left behind a widow, five sons and four daughters to follow his cortege to its final resting place, in the south aisle of All Saints, Fulham.

During her widowhood, Lady Mordaunt continued her friendship with Evelyn the diarist.

In August 1678 he writes...

> *"I went to my Lady Mordaunt, who*
> *put £100 into my hand to dispose*
> *of for pious uses, relief of prisoners,*
> *the poor etc., Many a sum has she*
> *sent me on similar occassions: a*
> *blessed creature she was ..."*

But her health began to fail and in July 1679 he sadly writes...

> *"14th July, I went to see how things*
> *stood at Parson's Green, My Lady*
> *Mordaunt (Now sick in Paris, wither*
> *she went for health) having made me*
> *a trustee for her children, an office I*
> *could not refuse."*

His good lady died shortly afterwards, leaving Evelyn to deal with the sale of the House at Parsons Green.

Her son, Charles inherited the estate and his father's titles, but in 1685 sold Reigate Priory to John Parsons, so ending the Mordaunt's connections with Reigate.

Sources

1. John Evelyn's Diaries
2. John Evelyn's Diaries
3. Papers at Reigate Priory
4. John Evelyn's Diaries
5. Edward Hyde, Lord Clarendon's Letters
6. State Trials
7. State Trials
8. State Trials
9. State Trials
10. State Trials
11. Samuel Pepys' Diaries
12. John Evelyn's Diaries
13. John Evelyn's Diaries

The Rogue

RYEGATE CHURCH, SURRY.

Published by J. Robson. New Bond Street Dec 1790.

Author's Notes

William Ridgeway wrote an unpublished
description of Reigate as it was at the end
of the 18th century beginning of the 19th.
It was from this work, which can be seen
at the Holmesdale Natural History Club or
the History Centre at Redhill Library, that
I obtained the clues to the whereabouts of
the house and mill belonging to Richard
Roades.
This manuscript makes interesting reading
as it names most of Reigate's house owners
street by street.

In 1696, with the Christmas festivities in full swing, Reigate was rocked by scandal.

A young woman named Anne Edwards had disappeared, much to the consternation of her friends in the town.

She had for some time worked for a merchant in Bell Lane, keeping house for him and his elderly father.

Her employer, Richard Roades or Rhodes, was born in Reigate in March 1648/49 and although little is known of his early life, by 1696 he had become a successful Oatmealman, supplying the meal for ship's biscuits to the Admiralty, from his premises in Bell Lane.

According to Ridgeway's unpublished history of Reigate, written in the first years of the 19th century, this house had been pulled down some time previously to make way for two houses, then owned by Messrs. Mansoll and Martyr, tailors.
Evidence points to the site being on the south corner of Bancroft Road and Bell Street.

Richard Roades, although in his forties was still a bachelor, which caused some talk when Anne first went to work for him, but it wasn't until Christmas 1696 that the scandal broke.

Anne Edwards vanished !

Her worried friends began to make enquiries as to her whereabouts, but her erstwhile employer denied all knowledge of her movements.

At this point there was talk of forming a search party to search the town and it was then that Richard Roades lost his nerve and fled the country, leaving a suspicion amongst Anne's friends that he was in some way responsible for her disappearance.

His house and gardens were searched and it was then that the body of poor Anne was discovered.

A 'Hue and cry' was raised against Roades but he was nowhere to be found.

Anne's funeral was held at St. Mary's on the 10th January 1696/7 and four days later a friend placed the following notice in the London Gazette...

[1]

> "Richard Rhodes of Rygate in Surry, Oatmeal Man, having in a barbarous manner Murdered Anne Edwards, his servant, is fled from justice, he is a thin man of Middle stature, long visage, light grey eyes often blood-shed, waering his own hair of a dark brown colour, curled at the end, and a scar from the corner of one of his eyes downwards aged about 40 years. Whoever can discover him, and cause him to be Apprehended, shall be well Rewarded by the Friend of the Deceased, living at Rygate aforesaid."

Then came one of those lucky breaks, which given that there was no national police force and no radio or television to spread the news, was nothing but miraculous.

An Englishman, passing through Drogheda, stoped at an inn for the night. When the waiter served his supper, the traveller was struck by the likeness he bore to the murderer of Anne Edwards, as described in the London Gazette, which he had recently read.

During the course of the evening he engaged the waiter in conversation, noting he had an English accent.

Before leaving the next morning the traveller managed to trick the waiter into writing his name. Instead of Francis Hatcher, the alias he was known by in Ireland, he wrote his real name, Richard Roades. Roades was immediately taken into custody and returned to England in chains.

He appeared at the Reigate Assizes, pleading guilty to the murder of Anne Edwards. In his confession he said that she had told him she was carrying his child and in the ensuing argument, he had killed her, burying the body in the back garden of his house in Bell Lane.

No sooner had the vedict been given than Henry Harvy of Reigate, was writing to Lord Somers to aquaint him with the news.

2

My Lord,

Receiving the Honour of Lord Thyn commands that I should aquaint your Lordship by leter with what happened of moment in your concerns in Rygate, I humbly presume on the liberty to inform your Lordship that one Richard Roades of Rygate was this Assises convicted of the barbarous murder committed there.

81

He was a man of considerable dealing
and it appeared in the evidence that a
dept of five hubdred pounds and upwards
is due from his Majesty in the Navy office,
besides which there are effects considerable,
to which by his conviction I presume, your
Lordship will be intitled. It also appeared
that he was in dept to several persons, but
not near the value of his estate. I am taking
care that his concerns here be secured and
shall then wait on your Lordship for your
comments herein to.

Your Lordships most
Obedent and Humbly
devoted servant

As the Lord of the manor, John Somers, who was also Lord Chancellor was entitled to the estate of any convicted felon living within the boundaries of Reigate and needless to say he took what he felt was his due.

Richard Roades was sentenced to be hanged at the scene of the crime, then as a deterrent to others, his body was to be hung in chains from a gibbet on the top of Red Hill.

Under cover of darkness the body disappeared.

This might have been the end of the matter, but according to Ridgeway's manuscript, in 1789 the owner of the Tanyard on Red Hill common, decided to build a pigsty.

To do this he had to take down a small fruit tree that was in his way and whilst digging up the roots, found a skeleton of a man he believed to be Richard Roades, as the previous owners of the Tanyard had been Roades' friends.

The body was reburied in the ground of what is now Earlswood Mount.

So ended a tragic incident in the history of Reigate.

Sources

1. The London Gazette.
2. Surrey History Centre, Woking, Surrey. Ref. 371/2/8/3 (2)

Bibliography

When I started my research the only books available on the history of Reigate were *Wilfred Hooper's - Reigate through the Ages* and *R.F.D. Palgrave's - A handbook to Reigate,* both of which were written well over 50 years ago, and are not always accurate in some of their basic assertions.

There are more books on the history of Surrey, the best of these are *Manning and Bray - History of Surrey,* which is in 3 volumes and *The Victoria County History -Surrey* in 4, but be warned, both of these are very large, very heavy reference works.

I also used the *Dictionary of National Biography* and the *Surrey Archaeological Collections* which can be found in the Redhill Library.

For the rest of the information, I had to go further afield, using primary sources from the following:

Public Records Office, Kew
Colindale Newspaper Library
The Surrey History Centre, Woking
Croydon Reference Library

For those interested in military history of the 17th century, I would recommend *C.H. Firth's - History of Cromwell's Army* and also his *Regimental History of Cromwell's Army* and any of the books by Brigadier Peter Young.

B-M.P.

Index

Places

Other books in the series

The History of Redhill Technical
School 1926-1966
Published January 2000

Tom Slaughter

Reigate and Redhill in Bygone Days
Published July 2000

Tony Powell

Redhill, Reigate and District
Family History Guide to Local
Records
To be published September/October 2000

Arthur Hawkes

Tudor Times in Reigate
To be published November/December 2000

Tony Powell